United States Government Accountability Office

Report to Congressional Requesters

I0448729

September 2013

CORPORATE TAX EXPENDITURES

Evaluations of Tax Deferrals and Graduated Tax Rates

GAO-13-789

GAO Highlights

Highlights of GAO-13-789, a report to congressional requesters

CORPORATE TAX EXPENDITURES

Evaluations of Tax Deferrals and Graduated Tax Rates

Why GAO Did This Study

Congress and the administration are reexamining tax expenditures used by corporations as part of corporate tax reform. These tax expenditures—special exemptions and exclusions, credits, deductions, deferrals, and preferential tax rates—support federal policy goals, but result in revenue forgone by the federal government.

GAO was asked to examine issues related to certain tax expenditures. This report uses GAO's tax expenditures evaluation guide to determine what is known about: (1) the deferral of income for controlled foreign corporations; (2) deferred taxes for certain financial firms on income earned overseas; and (3) the graduated corporate income tax rate. GAO combined the two deferral provisions for evaluation purposes.

GAO's guide suggests using five questions to evaluate a tax expenditure: (1) what is its purpose and is the purpose being achieved; (2) does it meet the criteria for good tax policy; (3) how is it related to other federal programs; (4) what are its consequences for the federal budget; and (5) how is its evaluation being managed? To address these questions, GAO reviewed the legislative history and relevant academic and government studies, analyzed 2010 Internal Revenue Service (IRS) data, and interviewed agency officials and tax experts.

What GAO Recommends

GAO made no recommendations. Treasury, IRS, the Joint Committee on Taxation, and external experts provided technical comments that were incorporated, as appropriate.

View GAO-13-789. For more information, contact James R. White at (202) 512-9110 or whitej@gao.gov.

What GAO Found

Deferral: Both deferral tax expenditures confer the benefit of effectively reducing taxes by delaying the taxation of certain income of foreign subsidiaries of U.S. corporations until it is repatriated to the U.S. parent as dividends.

1. While views on the purpose of deferral have changed over time, currently, it is often viewed by experts as promoting the competitiveness of U.S. multinational corporations. Some experts argue that this view is too narrow. For example, this definition of competitiveness ignores the effect on other corporations that cannot use deferral, such as those that are purely domestic or export without foreign subsidiaries. Further, it ignores impacts on the wider economy.
2. Good tax policy has several dimensions. By delaying the tax on foreign source income, deferral could distort corporate investment and location decisions in a way that lower taxes, but favor less productive activities over more productive ones. Informed judgments about deferral's effect on the fairness of the tax system cannot be made because who benefits from deferral, after accounting for such factors as changes in prices and wages, has not been determined. However, there is widespread agreement among experts and the Internal Revenue Service (IRS) that deferral adds complexity to the tax code.
3. GAO did not identify other federal spending programs that provide similar support to U.S. multinational corporations.
4. Joint Committee on Taxation (JCT) 2011 estimates show relatively modest consequences for the federal budget.
5. No federal agency has been tasked with evaluating deferral.

Graduated corporate income tax rate schedule: The graduated tax rates lower tax rates for corporations with less than $10 million in taxable income.

1. The purpose of the graduated corporate income tax rate schedule is viewed by the sources GAO reviewed as supporting small businesses. However, evidence is mixed on whether it achieves this purpose. The tax rates may not be well targeted toward supporting small businesses because corporations that are large in terms of assets and gross receipts may have taxable income that is small enough to qualify for the rates.
2. The economic efficiency of the graduated rates depends on whether they correct for a market failure. This includes too few small businesses forming, given their potential for profit and innovation, which offsets the possible distortions from its advantaging one type of business organization over others. GAO did not identify any studies of the efficiency effects or those that specifically estimate the distribution of the benefits from the graduated rates. According to IRS staff, while the graduated rates present little complexity, some evidence of tax planning to avoid higher rates has been found.
3. The graduated rates may be related to a number of federal spending programs also targeted to small businesses.
4. JCT 2011 estimates also show modest consequences for the federal budget.
5. No federal agency has been tasked with evaluating the graduated rates.

_____ **United States Government Accountability Office**

Contents

Letter		1
	Background	4
	Evaluation of Tax Deferrals	9
	Evaluation of Graduated Corporate Income Tax Rate Schedule	25
	Agency and Third Party Comments and Our Evaluation	35

Appendix I	Objectives, Scope, and Methodology	37

Appendix II	Comparison of Territorial and Worldwide Corporate Income Tax Systems	43

Appendix III	IRS Statistics of Income Data on the Number of C Corporations by Taxable Income and Size of Business Receipts, 2010	48

Appendix IV	GAO Contact and Staff Acknowledgments	50

Tables

Table 1: Corporate Income Tax Rate Schedule	7
Table 2: Percentage of Corporations with Positive Taxable Income by Taxable Income and Size of Business Receipts, 2010	28
Table 3: Number of Corporate Taxpayers by Taxable Income and Size of Business Receipts, 2010	48
Table 4: Coefficient of Variation Calculations for Totals in Table 3	49

Figures

Figure 1: Example of Deferral under the U.S. Worldwide Corporate Income Tax System	5
Figure 2: Ratio of U.S. Corporate Profits Earned Abroad to Total U.S. Corporate Profits, 1987-2012	23
Figure 3: Number of Returns by Form of Business, Tax Year 1986-2008	27

Figure 4: Estimated Federal Tax Revenue Losses Due to Graduated
     Corporate Income Tax Rate Schedule, Reported by
     Treasury, 1998-2012   34
Figure 5: Example of Worldwide and Territorial Corporate Income
     Tax Systems   44

Abbreviations

BEA	Bureau of Economic Analysis
CBO	Congressional Budget Office
CRS	Congressional Research Service
FTC	Foreign Tax Credit
IRC	Internal Revenue Code
IRS	Internal Revenue Service
JCT	Joint Committee on Taxation
OMB	Office of Management and Budget
SOI	Statistics of Income
Treasury	Department of the Treasury

GAO U.S. GOVERNMENT ACCOUNTABILITY OFFICE

441 G St. N.W.
Washington, DC 20548

September 16, 2013

The Honorable John Lewis
Ranking Member
Committee on Ways and Means
Subcommittee on Oversight
United States House of Representatives

The Honorable Lloyd Doggett
United States House of Representatives

In the past few years, both Congress and the administration have proposed reforming the corporate income tax system. A key component of discussions about reform is determining how the income of U.S. multinational corporations should be taxed—in particular, whether the federal government should continue or modify the current deferral of taxes on certain income until it is repatriated back to the United States. Currently, there are two provisions that relate to the deferral of U.S. taxation of foreign-source income: a general provision that applies to all controlled foreign corporations and a special provision applicable to active financial-services income. Another key component of reform discussions is the appropriate corporate income tax rate and structure. The current structure includes a set of graduated tax rates. The Department of the Treasury (Treasury) identifies both deferral provisions and the graduated rates as corporate tax expenditures because they are reductions in the federal corporate income tax liability that result from special provisions of the tax code. As our prior work pointed out, these tax expenditures are among the largest utilized only by corporate taxpayers.[1] According to Treasury's estimates, the amount of corporate tax revenue forgone from these three tax expenditures totaled almost $49 billion in fiscal year

---

[1]Our prior work highlighted a number of tax expenditures used by both corporate and individual taxpayers that had tax expenditure estimates that were larger or similar in size to the three tax expenditures covered in this report. See GAO, *Corporate Tax Expenditures: Information on Estimated Revenue Losses and Related Federal Spending Programs*, GAO-13-339 (Washington, D.C.: Mar. 18, 2013).

2012.[2] Modifying or eliminating these tax expenditures as part of corporate tax reform will likely involve tradeoffs between various objectives pursued by the federal government, such as tax revenue and corporate investment.

Because of your ongoing interest in whether and how well these tax expenditures are achieving their purposes, you requested that we apply the guide that we recently developed for evaluating the performance of tax expenditures to certain corporate ones.[3] This report uses our guide to determine what is known about the following three tax expenditures: (1) the deferral of income for controlled foreign corporations; (2) deferred taxes for certain financial firms on income earned overseas; and (3) the graduated corporate income tax rate.

Because the two deferral provisions are so similar, we combine them for evaluation purposes, and then evaluate the graduated rates separately.

Our tax expenditure evaluation guide outlines a series of questions and criteria that can be used to evaluate tax expenditures. The five primary questions outlined in the guide are:

1. What is the tax expenditure's purpose and is it being achieved?
2. Even if its purpose is achieved, is the tax expenditure good policy?

    a. Does it generate net economic benefits for society?

    b. Is it fair?

    c. Is it simple, transparent, and administrable?

---

[2]Corporate tax expenditure estimates totaled $147 billion in 2012 while corporate income tax revenue totaled $242 billion. Corporate tax expenditure estimates may be larger relative to corporate income tax revenues due to the continuing effects of a recovering economy as well as bonus depreciation, a temporary provision to stimulate investment, scheduled to expire at the end of 2013. While sufficiently reliable as a gauge of general magnitude, summing tax expenditure estimates does not take into account any interactions between tax expenditures. In addition, tax expenditure estimates do not incorporate any behavioral responses. Thus, they do not represent the revenue amount that would be gained if a specific tax expenditure was repealed.

[3]GAO, *Tax Expenditures: Background and Evaluation Criteria and Questions,* GAO-13-167SP (Washington, D.C.: Nov. 29, 2012). The graduated corporation income tax rate is the terminology used in Treasury's tax expenditure estimates, but we refer to it as the graduated corporate income tax rate schedule or graduated rates for this report.

GAO-13-789 Corporate Tax Expenditures

3. How does the tax expenditure relate to other federal programs?

4. What are the consequences for the federal budget of the tax expenditure?

5. How should evaluation of the tax expenditure be managed?

The guide's questions cover a number of different policy objectives, which sometimes compete with one another. This report provides information in response to the questions, but does not attempt to balance the different objectives or make recommendations. Rather, policymakers are in the best position to judge how competing policy objectives should be weighed.

As we note in our tax expenditure evaluation guide, the guide is not a "one size fits all" framework for evaluating tax expenditures. We used reasonable judgment in applying the guide's questions and concepts to evaluate the three tax expenditures. In some instances, we focused our discussion on certain questions in the guide because they were more relevant to the tax expenditures we were evaluating. At the same time, we devoted less discussion to other questions that were more technical in nature. See appendix I for the guide's full list of questions.

To determine what is known with respect to the deferral tax expenditures and the graduated corporate income tax rate schedule, we reviewed a variety of sources. These sources included studies by GAO, the Congressional Research Service (CRS), the Congressional Budget Office (CBO), the Joint Committee on Taxation (JCT), and other federal agencies; legislation, statutes, and regulations related to each of the tax expenditures; and academic research. We also interviewed officials at Treasury, the Internal Revenue Service (IRS), and three external experts, one from CRS and two from universities, who have researched and written extensively on the U.S. corporate income tax system. The results from these interviews are not generalizable. When no consensus existed among our sources for the answer to a question, we summarized the debate and provided citations for the various views. We analyzed Treasury's tax expenditure estimates from 1998 to 2012, and 2011 estimates by JCT on the revenue effects of changing tax expenditures. We also analyzed 2010 data from the IRS Statistics of Income (SOI), the most recent year available at the time of our work, and data from the Bureau of Economic Analysis (BEA) that covered 1987 to 2012. To assess the reliability of the data and estimates, we reviewed agency documentation, interviewed agency officials, and reviewed our prior reports that have used them. We determined that the Treasury, BEA,

JCT, and IRS data and estimates were sufficiently reliable for our purposes.[4]

We conducted our work from April to September 2013 in accordance with all sections of GAO's Quality Assurance Framework that are relevant to our objectives. The framework requires that we plan and perform the engagement to obtain sufficient and appropriate evidence to meet our stated objectives, and to discuss any limitations in our work. We believe that the information and data obtained, and the analysis conducted, provide a reasonable basis for any findings and conclusions in this product.

Background

The United States taxes domestic corporations on their worldwide income, regardless of where it is earned, and provides credits for foreign income taxes paid. A U.S. parent corporation may directly or indirectly own multiple corporations, including both domestic and foreign subsidiaries. The U.S. taxes the worldwide income of U.S. corporations, whether earned domestically or abroad. However, the active business income earned by foreign subsidiaries is generally eligible for deferral from U.S. tax until it is distributed, usually in the form of dividends, to the U.S. parent corporation or other U.S. shareholders.[5] When income is repatriated in this way, it may have already been taxed in the foreign country where it was earned. To avoid taxing foreign source income twice, the federal tax code allows U.S. parent corporations a foreign tax credit (FTC) for taxes paid to other countries. A U.S. corporation would pay U.S. tax on foreign-source income only to the extent that the U.S. tax on that income exceeds the FTC. Figure 1 shows how deferral affects how a dividend payment from a foreign subsidiary to its U.S. parent corporation is generally taxed under the U.S. worldwide tax approach.

[4]The SOI corporate sample is not designed to estimate the number of corporations in small subgroups with the exception of groups consisting of only large corporations. In addition, some cells with very small numbers are collapsed or suppressed to protect taxpayer information.

[5]Dividends are only one form of foreign source income. Others can include royalties, license payments, and export income. See CRS, *Moving to a Territorial Income Tax: Options and Challenges* (Washington, D.C.: July 25, 2012).

Figure 1: Example of Deferral under the U.S. Worldwide Corporate Income Tax System

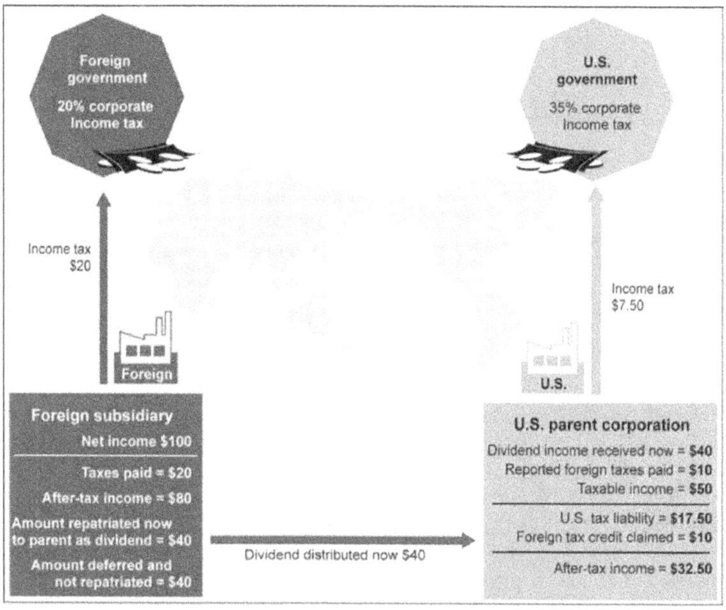

Source: GAO analysis.

Passive income, such as dividends, interest, rental income, and royalties received by controlled foreign corporations, and certain types of easily manipulated active income, is not subject to deferral.[6] Income ineligible for deferral is defined under Subpart F of the Internal Revenue Code (IRC).

Unlike the United States, most developed countries do not tax corporations on their worldwide income. Instead, these countries use a territorial tax system that taxes only the income earned within a country's physical borders, and exempts from tax dividends received from foreign subsidiaries on their foreign earnings as well as gains realized on the sale

---

[6]Lowell D. Yoder, "Subpart F in Turmoil: Low-Taxed Active Income Under Siege" *Taxes*, vol. 77 (March 1999).

of foreign subsidiaries. There has been a trend of developed countries moving towards territorial tax systems. As of 2012, 28 of the 34 current member countries of the Organisation for Economic Co-operation and Development have adopted some form of a territorial tax system.[7] However, most countries generally do not use a pure form of either the worldwide (also known as a full-inclusion system) or territorial tax system. Rather, countries tend to use a hybrid system that contains some features of both systems. For example, the deferral provisions in the U.S. worldwide system delay the taxation of foreign source income, whereas a purer form of the worldwide system would tax this income as it is earned. As we have previously found, countries using the territorial approach do not exempt all foreign source income from taxation, but have exceptions for certain types of passive income.[8]

The income of controlled foreign corporations that is generated through the primary business activities related to financial-services is excepted from Subpart F's anti-deferral regime. Interest income, for example, which would typically fall under the Subpart F definition, and thus would be taxed currently whether or not it is repatriated to a U.S. parent corporation, is permitted to be deferred under this active financial-services income provision. This tax expenditure is an exception to Subpart F because it treats what would otherwise be considered passive income as active business income that can be deferred since it was earned through the primary business activities of financial-services companies. The effect of the exception is to include financial-services companies among the U.S. corporations that can defer taxation on their business income earned abroad.

The United States taxes all foreign and domestic corporate income using a graduated corporate income tax rate structure. Corporations with less than $10 million in net taxable corporate income are subject to different tax rates, depending on the amount of income earned. As seen in table 1, income is taxed at graduated rates of 15, 25, 39, and 34 percent for

---

[7]PWC identified six countries that have a worldwide tax system with a foreign tax credit. These include the United States, Mexico, the Republic of Korea, Israel, Ireland, and Chile. See PWC, *Evolution of Territorial Tax Systems in the OECD*, prepared for the Technology CEO Council (Apr. 2, 2013).

[8]GAO, *International Taxation: Study Countries That Exempt Foreign-Source Income Face Compliance Risks and Burdens Similar to Those in the United States,* GAO-09-934 (Washington, D.C.: Sept. 15, 2009).

various income levels up to $10 million, and 35 and 38 percent for income up to $18,333,333. The 38- and 39-percent rates reduce the benefits provided by the lower graduated rates.[9] Finally, for corporations with taxable income higher than $18,333,333, a flat rate of 35 percent applies to all taxable income.

Table 1: Corporate Income Tax Rate Schedule

Taxable Income over	But not over...	Tax rate	Of the amount over...
$0	$50,000	15%	$0
$50,000	$75,000	$7,500 + 25%	$50,000
$75,000	$100,000	13,750 + 34%	$75,000
$100,000	$355,000	22,250 + 39%	$100,000
$335,000	$10,000,000	113,900 + 34%	$335,000
$10,000,000	$15,000,000	3,400,000 + 35%	$10,000,000
$15,000,000	$18,333,333	5,150,000 + 38%	$15,000,000
$18,333,333	-	35%	0

Source: Internal Revenue Service.

Treasury and JCT designate the two deferral provisions and the graduated corporate income tax rate schedule as tax expenditures because they are special tax provisions that are exceptions to the normal structure of the corporate income tax system.[10] The deferral provisions are designated as tax expenditures because they deviate from the baseline case of a pure worldwide tax system in which U.S. corporations would be taxed on their worldwide income whether or not the income is repatriated to the United States. The graduated rate provision is designated a tax expenditure because it is an exception to the normal structure of a flat corporate income tax rate. All three tax expenditures

---

[9]Once reached, the two highest brackets give corporations an average tax rate of 34 and 35 percent, respectively.

[10]The concept of tax expenditures extends beyond the income tax. Tax expenditures also exist for other types of taxes, such as excise and payroll taxes. However, this report considers only tax expenditures for the federal income tax system. Different tax expenditures would apply in the case of a consumption tax.

GAO-13-789 Corporate Tax Expenditures

reduce revenue received by the federal government below what it would be under the normal structure established by Treasury and JCT.[11]

Treasury and JCT each compile an annual list of tax expenditures by budget function with estimates of the corporate and individual income tax revenue losses, also known as tax expenditure estimates.[12] They separately calculate the estimated revenue losses for each tax expenditure under the assumptions that all other tax expenditures remain in the tax code, and taxpayer behavior remains constant.[13] Thus, the tax expenditure estimates do not represent the amount of revenue that would be gained if a particular tax expenditure was repealed, since repeal would probably change taxpayer behavior in some way that would affect revenue.

---

[11]Both Treasury and JCT use judgment when establishing their normal baseline tax structures. It is sometimes the case that a particular provision is considered an exception to the baseline structure and another, very similar provision is not. For example, graduated rates for C corporations are considered an exception, while S corporation provisions that can also provide lower tax rates for businesses are not. Treasury also discusses an alternative baseline tax structure—the reference tax baseline—which defines as tax expenditures only those provisions that are special exceptions from a generally defined tax rule that serves programmatic functions similar to spending programs. The general deferral provision and the graduated rates are not considered to be tax expenditures relative to this baseline. In addition, in 2008, JCT did not consider either of the deferral provisions as tax expenditures under a new approach for considering tax expenditures used only in that year. See JCT, *Estimates of Federal Tax Expenditures for Fiscal Years 2008-2027*, JCS-2-08 (Washington, D.C.: Oct. 31, 2008).

[12]Office of Management and Budget (OMB), *Analytical Perspectives, Budget of the United States Government, Fiscal Year 2014* (Washington, D.C.: 2013); and JCT, *Estimates of Federal Tax Expenditures for Fiscal Years 2012-2017*, JCS-1-13 (Washington, D.C.: Feb. 1, 2013).

[13]While, in general, the tax expenditure lists Treasury and JCT publish annually are similar, they differ somewhat in the number of tax expenditures reported, and the estimated revenue losses for particular expenditures. The organizations use different (1) income tax baselines; (2) de minimis amounts, which is the minimum revenue loss threshold for Treasury and JCT to report a tax expenditure; and (3) economic and technical assumptions. For more information on how Treasury and JCT estimate revenue loss, see appendix III of GAO, *Government Performance and Accountability: Tax Expenditures Represent a Substantial Federal Commitment and Need to Be Reexamined*, GAO-05-690 (Washington, D.C.: Sept. 23, 2005).

Evaluation of Tax Deferrals

1 What is the tax expenditure's purpose and is it being achieved?

Deferral Is Viewed by Many as Promoting Competitiveness

Deferral has long been a part of the tax code, and views of its purpose have changed over time. Currently, it is often viewed by tax experts and in the research that we reviewed as promoting competitiveness.[14] However, deferral's effect on competitiveness depends on how competitiveness is defined. If competitiveness refers to the ability of U.S. multinational corporations to operate successfully in foreign markets through their subsidiaries, then deferral, which increases after tax returns by delaying tax payments, provides a benefit that may enhance competitiveness.[15] In foreign markets, U.S. corporations face competitors that, operating under a territorial tax system in their own countries, pay

---

[14]As the Congressional Research Service (CRS) points out in its tax expenditures compendium, deferral has been part of the U.S. tax system since the creation of the corporate income tax in 1909. See U.S. Congress, Senate Committee on the Budget, *Tax Expenditures: Compendium of Background Material on Individual Provisions*, S. Prt. 111-58, prepared by CRS (Washington, D.C.: December 2012). Initially, the deferral of tax on the income of controlled foreign corporations may have been meant to delay taxation until a corporation realized income, according to the notion that income should not be taxed before it is available for taxpayer use.

[15]Competitiveness has been identified as the purpose of deferral in parts of the legislative history. Subsequent legislative changes, primarily during the creation of Subpart F, provided a more explicit purpose for deferral. While considering how to restrict deferral through Subpart F in 1962, as well as creating the exception for deferred taxes for certain income earned overseas by financial-services firms, both the House and Senate reports recognized deferral was needed to help maintain active American business operations abroad on an equal competitive footing with other businesses operating overseas. See H.R. Rep. No. 87-1447, 62 (1962); S. Rep. No. 87-1881, at 83 (1962). See also H.R. Conf. Rep. No. 105-220 644-45 (1997). Changes in Subpart F were also introduced to encourage investment in less developed countries. See Treasury, *The Deferral of Income Earned Through U.S. Controlled Foreign Corporations: A Policy Study* (Washington, D.C.: December 2000).

GAO-13-789 Corporate Tax Expenditures

tax only in the foreign country. U.S. corporations under the worldwide system must pay the foreign tax plus any U.S. tax on the same income. By delaying this U.S. tax, deferral is said to move U.S. corporations closer to having a "level playing field" with their foreign competitors.

Whether the tax benefit provided by deferral results in net positive economic effects for the United States is the subject of debate. Some research has found that investments U.S. multinationals make abroad, due in part to the incentives provided by deferral, lead to positive economic effects for employment and wages in the United States, while others have questioned the magnitude of these effects.[16] Treasury officials noted that in some instances U.S. foreign direct investment may be associated with increased investment in the United States. In other instances, it may be associated with decreased U.S. investment, meaning that the effect on employment and wages in the United States would be uncertain.

However, whether this definition of competitiveness that focuses on multinationals is appropriate has been a subject of debate among experts.[17] Competitiveness has also been defined as the ability of U.S. corporations to operate successfully in domestic markets, and to export products into foreign markets. Deferral provides no benefit to these purely domestic or exporting U.S corporations. Rather than leveling the playing field, deferral benefits U.S. multinationals over other types of U.S. corporations.[18] Our prior work has shown that deferral and other aspects

---

[16]Other factors, such as differences in regulatory and trade frameworks, may provide incentives to invest abroad as well. See Mihir A. Desai, C. Fritz Foley, and James R. Hines Jr., "Domestic Effects of the Foreign Activities of U.S. Multinationals," *American Economic Journal: Economic Policy* (2009), Martin Sullivan, "Economic Analysis: Will Obama's International Proposals Kill U.S. Jobs?", *Tax Notes Today* (June 1, 2009), and Harry Grubert, "Foreign Taxes and The Growing Share of U.S. Multinational Company Income Abroad: Profits, Not Sales, Are Being Globalized," *National Tax Journal*, vol. 65 (June 2012).

[17]See Nicola Satori and Reuven S. Avi-Yonah, "Symposium on International Taxation and Competitiveness: Foreword," *Tax Law Review*, vol. 65 (Spring 2012). This paper summarizes a variety of viewpoints on competitiveness.

[18]A number of tax expenditures benefit U.S. corporations that produce domestically, such as the inventory property sales source rules exception and the deduction for U.S. production activities, although both have tax expenditure estimates smaller than the general deferral provision. See OMB, *Analytical Perspectives, Budget of the United States Government, Fiscal Year 2014* (Washington, D.C.: 2013).

of U.S. international corporate taxation allow U.S. multinational corporations to pay a much smaller U.S. effective tax rate on foreign source income than domestic income.[19] If these multinationals earn income in countries that, on average, have lower corporate tax rates than the United States, they have an advantage over purely domestic U.S. corporations because the average effective tax rate on the multinationals' worldwide income may be lower than the rate paid by the purely domestic corporations on their U.S. income. However, there is some research that has found that multinationals and domestic-only firms face similar effective tax rates.[20]

Other tax experts argue that the appropriate definition of competitiveness should focus on broader industry or national purposes rather than corporations.[21] For example, a U.S. industry is said to be more competitive by attracting more investment and resources than foreign industries.[22] For others, competitiveness is a more general concept, referring to the set of institutions, policies, and human and natural endowments that make a country productive. A tax policy that promotes competitiveness under this definition would try to assure that the tax system does not prevent a country's resources from being put to their most productive uses.[23] Countries that meet this standard can engage most effectively in international trade that can be mutually beneficial. Tax benefits for only certain corporations or industries may not meet this criterion. Finally, some experts note that the concept of competitiveness is the wrong concept to focus on when formulating tax policy and that efficiency, which we discuss in the following section, is the appropriate

---

[19]GAO, *U.S. Multinational Corporations: Effective Tax Rates Are Correlated with Where Income Is Reported*, GAO-08-950 (Washington, D.C.: Aug. 12, 2008). Deferral reduces U.S. multinational corporations' effective tax rate. The present value of a tax paid in the future is generally less than that of a tax paid today because the taxpayer can then use the funds (for example, for investment) until the tax is paid. These funds would have been unavailable to the taxpayer had the tax been paid earlier.

[20] See Kevin S. Markle and Douglas Shackelford, "Do Multinationals or Domestic Firms Face Higher Effective Tax Rates?," *National Bureau of Economic Research Working Paper Series* (June 2009).

[21]See Eric Toder, "International Competitiveness: Who Competes Against Whom and for What?," *Tax Law Review*, vol. 65 (Spring 2012).

[22]See Michael S. Knoll, "The Connection Between Competitiveness and International Taxation," *Tax Law Review*, vol. 65 (Spring 2012).

[23]The concept of economic efficiency is described in more detail later in this report.

concept. They argue that simply using the wrong concept in this way leads to bad policy outcomes.[24]

2 Even if its purpose is achieved, is the tax expenditure good policy?

- Does the tax expenditure generate net economic benefits for society?
- Is the tax expenditure fair?
- Is the tax expenditure simple, transparent, and administrable?

Numerous Business Decisions Are Affected by Deferral and Each Has Consequences for Efficiency

Tax differences between countries can affect decisions made by multinational corporations, including where to invest in operations, where to locate their corporate residences, when to repatriate income from foreign subsidiaries, and whether to acquire foreign or domestic corporations. Their decisions are said to be distorted when the corporations respond to tax differences by putting resources into less productive activities because these activities are taxed less heavily than more productive uses. As we stated in our guide, when this happens, the economy is not as productive as it could be, and society does not achieve as high a standard of living as it would if the distortion did not exist.[25]

As mentioned above, the United States uses a hybrid form of the worldwide tax system where deferral delays but does not eliminate the U.S. tax on foreign source income. In this way, the U.S. worldwide system has some features less like a pure worldwide system and more like a territorial system. Moving in either direction would affect deferral. On one hand, the United States could eliminate deferral if it moved towards a more pure worldwide system by adopting a full inclusion system where foreign source income is taxed by the United States as it is earned rather than when it is repatriated. On the other hand, the United States could move towards a more territorial system by exempting foreign source

---

[24]See Jane G. Gravelle, "Does the Concept of Competitiveness Have Meaning in Formulating Corporate Tax Policy?," *Tax Law Review*, vol. 65 (Spring 2012).

[25]See GAO-13-167SP for a more detailed discussion of economic efficiency. Also see appendix II of this report for an example of how these inefficiencies can occur when taxes affect how taxpayers make investment decisions.

income from U.S. taxation, or, in effect, making deferral permanent.[26] The effect on corporations' decision making and ultimately on efficiency will depend on which way of ending deferral is adopted. The following discusses some of the decisions that have been identified in the literature where deferral could increase or decrease distortions.

Some tax experts argue that deferral may distort decisions about where U.S. corporations invest, compared to a full-inclusion system, if the U.S. tax rate is higher than foreign tax rates, as is often the case. This difference in tax rates, combined with the ability to defer paying the higher U.S. tax until income is repatriated, could mean that a U.S. corporation earns more after taxes from a less productive investment abroad than from a more productive investment at home. The efficiency loss is the loss of income (or product) that results when the corporation chooses the less productive foreign investment because it produces a higher after-tax return. Some research has shown that differences in tax burden do affect corporations' real investment decisions, which could lead to these efficiency losses.[27] If the United States adopted a full inclusion system, this distortion affecting the allocation of investment domestically or abroad could potentially be reduced because the tax incentive to invest abroad would be eliminated, since corporations would pay the same U.S. tax on their worldwide income, whether it comes from foreign or domestic investments. Under a territorial system, these investment location distortions may increase relative to the current system because the tax incentive to invest in low-tax countries may be enhanced when the differences in tax rates are made permanent. However, the responsiveness of investment decisions to tax rate differences indicates that U.S. corporations could be at a disadvantage under a full inclusion system as they could be competing against foreign companies which would likely be taxed under a territorial tax system and at a lower tax rate. This disadvantage would be removed under a territorial system where U.S. corporations would face the same tax rate as foreign competitors also operating in those countries.

---

[26]CRS, among others, outlined a number of other considerations that may have to be evaluated if a move to a territorial tax system was implemented. CRS, *Moving to a Territorial Income Tax: Options and Challenges* (Washington, D.C.: July 15, 2012).

[27]Organisation for Economic Co-operation and Development, *Tax Effects on Foreign Direct Investment: Recent Evidence and Policy Analysis: Tax Policy Study No. 17* (2007).

Some experts and research that we reviewed argue that deferral may reduce distortions, compared to a full inclusion system, about where businesses decide to incorporate, and whether U.S. corporations choose to change their country of incorporation to a foreign country (so-called corporate inversions). By choosing not to have its corporate residence in the U.S., a corporation could permanently avoid U.S. tax on income earned abroad, and whatever income it is able to shift out of the U.S. Deferral may somewhat reduce this distortion by allowing corporations to defer from tax income earned abroad. Some research has indicated that taxing income, once it is repatriated, affects decisions of where to incorporate, or to change incorporation from one country to another.[28] Some research has also shown that most inversions that occur for tax reasons are to avoid U.S. tax on income earned in the U.S. by increasing the scope for income shifting rather than to avoid U.S. tax on foreign-source income.[29] However, recent research has found mixed results on trends in the number of inversions. Some have found that only a small number of U.S. corporations that conduct initial public offerings have reincorporated in low-tax countries, while others have recently highlighted an increase in inversions.[30] In 2004, legislation was passed to limit the ability of U.S. corporations to change their country of incorporation to a foreign country.[31] This corporate residence distortion could be increased by full inclusion, which would raise the effective U.S. tax on income earned abroad, and encourage companies to avoid this tax by moving their residence abroad. A territorial system would eliminate this incentive by removing the U.S. tax on foreign source income.

---

[28]Change of incorporation may occur through a corporate inversion or cross-border merger and acquisition. See Johannes Voget, "Relocation of Headquarters and International Taxation," *Journal of Public Economics*, vol. 95 (October 2011).

[29]Jim A. Seida and William F. Wempe, "Effective Tax Rate Changes and Earning Stripping Following Corporate Inversion," *National Tax Journal*, vol. 57 (December 2004).

[30]Eric J. Allen and Susan C. Morse, "Tax-Haven Incorporation For U.S.-Headquartered Firms: No Exodus Yet," *National Tax Journal*, vol. 66 (June 2013); Martin Sullivan, "Economic Analysis: Another Pharmaceutical Inversion to Ireland; More on the Horizon?", *Tax Notes Today* (Aug. 8, 2013); and Bret Wells, "Cant and the Inconvenient Truth About Corporate Inversions," *Tax Notes Today* (July 5, 2012).

[31]The American Jobs Creation Act of 2004 (P.L. 108-357) was targeted at restricting corporate inversion. See CRS, *Firms That Incorporate Abroad for Tax Purposes: Corporate "Inversions" and "Expatriation"* (Washington, D.C.: Mar. 5, 2010).

It is also argued that deferral, compared to a full inclusion system, improves economic efficiency by removing distortions that affect decisions about which subsidiaries and other assets corporations own.[32] Some corporate groups may be able to use foreign subsidiaries and assets more productively because of synergies that result from ownership within the corporate group, while another corporate group that acquired these subsidiaries and assets would not have these synergies and therefore would not be able to use them as productively. For this reason, tax differences could lead to productivity loss when a corporation without those synergies, but with more favorable tax treatment is able to outbid for ownership of those assets a corporation with those synergies. In this case, the use of deferral or a territorial system makes inefficiency less likely and the move to full inclusion makes it more likely. However, others argue that ownership synergies do not have significant effects on productivity because there are numerous ways for corporations to use assets as productively without owning them, such as leasing, contract manufacturing, or licensing of trademarks or technology.[33] In this case, deferral or a move to a territorial system would not produce significant efficiency gains.

Some research has also shown that deferral can distort decision making by affecting the timing of repatriations, referred to as the "lockout" effect. The distortion would happen if deferral incentivizes corporations to keep income abroad rather than repatriating it to the higher tax country. This income may be more productive if repatriated and reinvested at home rather than retained (or "locked out") abroad for tax reasons. Although estimates have varied over time, they consistently show that the lockout effect does have efficiency costs. Estimates from 2001 of the efficiency cost of U.S. multinational corporations from the lockout effect put the size of the loss at about 1 percent of foreign pretax income.[34] However, the large repatriations under the 2004 tax holiday have suggested to some

---

[32]Mihir A. Desai and James Hines, "Evaluating International Tax Reform," *National Tax Journal*, vol. 46 (September 2003).

[33]CRS, *Reform of U.S. International Taxation: Alternatives* (Washington, D.C.: Dec. 27, 2012).

[34]Mihir A. Desai, C. Fritz Foley, and James R. Hines, "Repatriation Taxes and Dividend Distortions," *National Tax Journal,* vol. 54 (December 2001); and Harry Grubert and John Mutti, *Taxing International Business Income: Dividend Exemption versus the Current System* (Washington, D.C.: American Enterprise Institute) (2001).

researchers that these earlier estimates may be too small.[35] More recent estimates have shown that the efficiency loss increases with the amount of earnings accumulated abroad, and could be as high as 7 percent of foreign pretax income by 2015.[36] Both the territorial and full inclusion systems eliminate the lockout effect. The territorial system makes foreign earnings tax free whether or not they are repatriated, and the full inclusion system makes foreign earnings taxable without repatriation.

The extensive literature on deferral disagrees on its overall impact on efficiency, or whether a movement toward a full inclusion or territorial system would improve efficiency. Deferral's effect on the decisions just discussed, where to invest, where to locate headquarters, whether to make an acquisition, and when to repatriate income can depend on factors such as the location of the market (domestic or foreign) and the source of investment capital (again, domestic or foreign). In addition, there may be empirical disagreement about the size of an effect. Without agreement on the separate effects on efficiency, there is no agreement about how to add them up to get an overall effect.

2   **Even if its purpose is achieved, is the tax expenditure good policy?**

• Does the tax expenditure generate net economic benefits for society?
• **Is the tax expenditure fair?**
• Is the tax expenditure simple, transparent, and administrable?

Informed Judgments about Deferral's Equity Require Information about Ultimate Beneficiaries

We were unable to find any studies that specifically estimate the distribution of the benefits from the two deferral tax expenditures. Treasury, CBO, and the Tax Policy Center have developed estimates of the distribution of the corporate tax burden as a whole. However, these studies may not indicate who ultimately benefits from deferral and, further, whether deferral is fair and equitable.

---

[35]The American Jobs Creation Act of 2004, section 422, allowed companies to pay a one-time 5.25-percent tax rate on repatriated foreign earnings. Companies brought back $312 billion into the United States due to this change. See IRS, *The One-Time Received Dividend Deduction*, SOI Bulletin (Spring 2008).

[36]Harry Grubert and Rosanne Altshuler, *Fixing the System: An Analysis of Alternative Proposals for the Reform of International Tax*, Working Papers Series (Apr. 1, 2013).

The distribution of ultimate beneficiaries, referred to as the economic incidence of the tax benefit, depends on the extent that the tax provision leads to changes in the prices of goods or services. For example, the tax benefit for corporations from deferral may be passed on to consumers through lower prices, to employees through higher wages, or to investors through higher returns. Economic incidence is difficult to determine due to the complexity of the interactions that produce these price and income changes. Studies of the distribution of burdens and benefits usually base their estimates of economic incidence on empirical studies of how prices in relevant markets, including markets for goods and services or labor and capital markets, respond to changes in certain tax provisions. The studies of the corporate tax burden that we identified did not estimate the effect of deferral and their methods may require adjustments before such an estimate can be made. Without these estimates, informed judgments about deferral's fairness will be hard to draw because such judgments depend on knowing who receives the benefit of the tax expenditure. Equally, the distributional effects of the territorial and full inclusion alternatives to deferral are also unknown, and informed judgments about the fairness of the alternatives cannot be made.

Although the ultimate beneficiaries are unknown, there is some evidence that certain industries benefit more from deferral than others. An IRS study found that during the one-time U.S. repatriation tax holiday in 2004, certain industries, such as companies involved in pharmaceutical manufacturing and computer and electronic equipment manufacturing, benefited disproportionately, as they repatriated significantly more income in the form of dividends relative to the size of the tax filers.[37]

---

[37] See IRS, *The One-Time Received Dividend Deduction*, SOI Bulletin (Spring 2008).

Even if its purpose is achieved, is the tax expenditure good policy?

• Does the tax expenditure generate net economic benefits for society?
• Is the tax expenditure fair?
• Is the tax expenditure simple, transparent, and administrable?

Deferral Adds Complexity to the Tax Code

There is widespread agreement among tax experts that the U.S. system for taxing foreign source income is complex and adds burden for IRS and taxpayers. Deferral contributes to this complex system by enhancing the incentive for corporations to shift income abroad to be taxed at lower rates. Deferral further adds complexity by interacting with a number of tax provisions designed to limit income shifting.[38] One of those provisions, Subpart F of the IRC, creates an exception to the general rule of deferral by defining certain types of passive income, such as interest and royalties, as well as certain other easily manipulated income, as ineligible for deferral. These types of income are viewed as subject to greater manipulation to reduce taxes because they can be artificially shifted between related parties.[39] Moreover, there are also exceptions to Subpart F. As noted previously, interest income that is generated through the primary business activities of financial-services companies of controlled foreign corporations is eligible for deferral. These various provisions add complexity as taxpayers must determine which income can be deferred.

Deferral also affects complexity by interacting with the foreign tax credit and transfer pricing. Our prior work has highlighted these areas as major

---

[38]Most experts agree that the scope for income shifting and the resulting compliance and administrative burden have increased by the check-the-box regulations and the look-through provision of the IRC. The check-the-box regulations, issued by Treasury in 1997, permit U.S. taxpayers to treat certain wholly owned foreign entities either as separate corporations or to "disregard" them as unincorporated branches simply by checking a box on a tax form. Taxpayers have used this flexibility to create "hybrid entities," which are business operations treated as corporations by one country's tax authority, and as unincorporated branch operations by another's. See 26 C.F.R. §§ 301.7701-1 to 4. Congress passed the look-through rules in 2006. The rules allow dividends, interest, rents, and royalties received or accrued by one controlled foreign corporation from a related controlled foreign corporation not to be treated as Subpart F income and thus eligible for deferral. See 26 U.S.C. § 954(c)(6).

[39]The complexity of Subpart F has increased with the inclusion of the check-the-box regulations and the look-through rules discussed above.

sources of compliance risk and burden.[40] Deferral allows corporations to time their repatriations of foreign source income for periods when they have excess foreign tax credits, which can be used to lower the amount of U.S. tax they pay. In these cases, complex rules for determining the source of income are required to ensure that the foreign tax credits are applied only against the portion of the corporation's worldwide taxable income attributable to foreign sources.[41] Transfer pricing rules attempt to limit income shifting by requiring that related corporations charge prices for the goods and services they sell to each other that are comparable to market prices. Identifying and evaluating these transfer prices can be difficult for IRS and taxpayers when, as often is the case with intangible property, limited information exists on comparable market prices.

3   How does the tax expenditure relate to other federal programs?

Deferral Does Not Overlap Directly with Other Federal Programs

Our prior work on corporate tax expenditures identified no related federal activities sharing the same reported purpose as the two deferral tax expenditures.[42] Although we have highlighted export promotion programs as an area of potential duplication and overlap, these programs are focused primarily on small companies rather than U.S. multinational

---

[40]GAO, *International Taxation: Study Countries That Exempt Foreign-Source Income Face Compliance Risks and Burdens Similar to Those in the United States*, GAO-09-934 (Washington, D.C.: Sept. 15, 2009).

[41]The foreign tax credit also adds complexity when U.S. corporations try to time their repatriations to claim as much of the credit as possible. Corporations can lower the amount of U.S. tax they would otherwise have to pay by repatriating income from low-tax countries when they have excess foreign tax credits. The corporation uses cross-crediting where it applies excess foreign tax credits generated in a high-tax country to the U.S. tax owed on income generated in a low-tax country. Corporations, however, are not allowed to use excess credits associated with passive income to offset taxes on active income, or vice versa.

[42]See GAO-13-339.

corporations.[43] Deferral is integral to the way the United States taxes multinational corporations, and interacts with a number of other tax provisions, such as Subpart F. When considering reform to this system, changes to deferral would need to be coordinated with changes to other tax provisions.

4 What are the consequences of the federal budget of the tax expenditure?

Deferral May Have Relatively Modest Consequences for the Federal Budget but Estimates Vary

According to JCT estimates produced in 2011 and reported by CBO, ending deferral by moving to a full inclusion worldwide system, where foreign source income is taxed whether or not repatriated, would increase federal revenues by $4.7 billion in 2012. According to the same estimates, exempting active foreign dividends from U.S. tax, similar to that of a territorial tax system, and changing the tax treatment of overhead expenses would increase revenues by $3.3 billion in 2012.[44] These estimates are based on specific proposals to change the tax code,

---

[43]GAO, *2013 Annual Report: Actions Needed to Reduce Fragmentation, Overlap, and Duplication and Achieve Other Financial Benefits*, GAO-13-279SP (Washington, D.C.: Apr. 9, 2013).

[44]Over the 5-period from 2012 to 2016, CBO reports that the total estimated revenue effects of moving to a full inclusion worldwide system would be $49.7 billion, while the effect of moving to a territorial system would be $31.7 billion. These estimates were prepared for the CBO report by staff of JCT. For more details on the estimates, see CBO, *Reducing the Deficit: Spending and Revenue Options* (Washington, D.C.: Mar. 10, 2011). If estimates of the revenue effects of moving to a worldwide tax system more current than CBO's 2011 estimates were made, there is some evidence that they could be larger. JCT's tax expenditure estimates increased substantially after this revenue estimate was made, increasing from $15.6 billion to $36.6 billion in constant 2012 dollars. Although, as pointed out earlier, tax expenditure estimates do not include behavioral responses, the increase in the tax expenditure estimate may indicate a larger revenue impact if the U.S. moved to a full inclusion worldwide system.

and include behavioral responses by taxpayers to the tax change.[45] The revenue estimate for exempting active foreign dividends shows an increase in revenue chiefly because the expense allocation rules under this option reduced the expenses that can be deducted from U.S. income relative to the current system's expense allocation rules.[46]

The effect on U.S. tax revenue of full inclusion and territoriality depends on the incentives the alternatives provide to shift income out of the United States and its taxing authority and the specifics of the alternatives' design. The incentive to locate income in low-tax countries may be less under full inclusion and higher under the territorial system, thereby eroding the U.S. corporate tax base.[47] However, territorial systems in practice include design features, such as a minimum tax on foreign source income, that are intended to limit these losses.

JCT and Treasury also make tax expenditure estimates on a regular basis that do not account for how taxpayer behavior may change when a tax expenditure is altered. Although these estimates do not represent the

---

[45]JCT notes that its corporate tax model for estimating revenue effects includes possible behavioral changes in: (1) corporate dividends and retained earnings; (2) the corporate capital structure; (3) corporate equity valuations; (4) repatriations of deferred foreign income; and (5) business entity choice. See JCT, *Summary of Economic Models and Estimating Practices of the Staff of the Joint Committee on Taxation.* (Washington, D.C.: Sept. 19, 2011). JCT's revenue estimates prepared for specific proposals differ from its and Treasury's tax expenditure estimates that do not incorporate such behavioral responses. For an explanation of how JCT and Treasury complete their tax expenditure estimates, see JCT, *Estimates of Federal Tax Expenditures for Fiscal Years 2012-2017*, JCS-1-13 (Washington, D.C.: Feb. 1, 2013), and OMB, *Analytical Perspectives, Budget of the United States Government*, Fiscal Year 2014 (Washington, D.C.: 2013).

[46]Overhead costs, such as interest expenses, of a U.S. parent corporation would be allocated between the company's U.S. and foreign activities, as is the case under current law for purposes of computing the foreign tax credit. In a departure from current law, however, overhead expenses allocated to foreign income would no longer be deductible from U.S. income. As noted by CBO, the net increase in revenues when the dividend exemption system is adopted occurs because revenues lost by exempting active dividends from U.S. taxation would be more than offset by increases in taxes because overhead expenses allocated to exempt foreign income could no longer be deducted from U.S. income. If the tax treatment of overhead expenses was not altered, moving to a dividend exemption system may entail a reduction in the tax revenue the federal government collects from corporations.

[47]GAO, *International Taxation: Study Countries That Exempt Foreign-Source Income Face Compliance Risks and Burdens Similar to Those in the United States*, GAO-09-934 (Washington, D.C.: Sept. 15, 2009).

amount of revenue that would be gained if deferral were eliminated, they can indicate how revenue losses may be changing over time. The tax expenditure estimates show that revenue losses from the general deferral tax expenditure have increased significantly.[48] These estimates of increasing tax revenue losses are consistent with changes in the location of earnings of U.S. corporations. During this period, U.S. corporations were earning an increasing share of their profits from foreign sources, likely increasing the amount of income deferred abroad. As seen in figure 2, U.S. corporate profits earned abroad, compared to total U.S. corporate profits, have increased moderately since 1997.

---

[48]Treasury estimated that revenue losses from the deferral of income for controlled foreign corporations rose from about $7.7 billion in 1999 to $42 billion in 2012. The difference in the estimation methods is illustrated by the 2012 estimated revenue loss of $42 billion, and JCT's estimate of a $4.7 billion revenue gain for a specific proposal to adopt full inclusion. Estimates for deferred taxes for financial firms on certain income earned overseas during a similar period show revenue losses increasing at a slower pace, from $1.3 billion to $2.5 billion during the same period. As we pointed out in our prior work on corporate tax expenditures, the general deferral provision was the second largest in terms of tax expenditure estimates, behind only accelerated depreciation of machinery and equipment. See GAO-13-339.

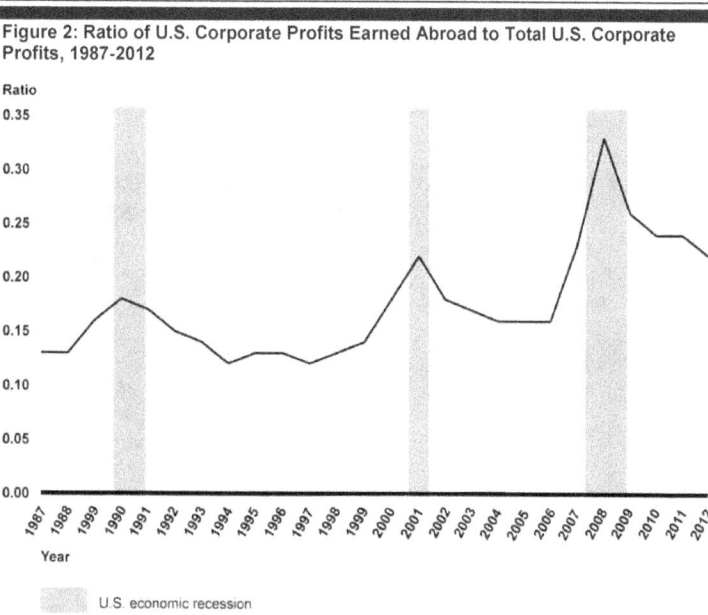

Figure 2: Ratio of U.S. Corporate Profits Earned Abroad to Total U.S. Corporate Profits, 1987-2012

U.S. economic recession

Ratio of U.S. corporate profits earned abroad to total corporate profits

Source: GAO analysis of Bureau of Economic Analysis data.

In addition, a number of legislative changes may have affected the revenue losses from deferral by making it easier to shift or keep income abroad. These include the look-through rule exception from Subpart F. This rule provides that dividends, interest, rents, and royalties received or accrued by one controlled foreign corporation from a related controlled foreign corporation are not treated as Subpart F income, and are eligible for deferral.[49] Finally, some have suggested that in light of the U.S. tax repatriation holiday in 2004, which allowed U.S. corporations to exempt most dividends from tax on a one-time basis, U.S. multinational

---

[49]The Tax Increase Prevention and Reconciliation Act ("TIPRA") of 2005 (H.R. 4297), enacted on May 17, 2006 (Pub. L. No. 109-222).

corporations may have accumulated foreign earnings abroad in anticipation of another repatriation holiday.[50]

5 How should evaluation of the tax expenditures be managed?

No Consensus Exists on Which Agency Should Evaluate Deferral

No federal agency has been tasked to evaluate deferral. Since 1994, we have recommended greater scrutiny of tax expenditures, as periodic reviews could help determine how well specific tax expenditures work to achieve their goals, and how their benefits and costs compare to those of programs with similar goals.[51] However, as we reported in June 2013, the Office of Management and Budget (OMB) has not developed a framework for reviewing tax expenditure performance.[52] We made a number of recommendations to OMB, including that it provide guidance to agencies to identify tax expenditures that contribute to each appropriate agency goal. In July 2013, OMB released guidance that directs agencies to identify tax expenditures that contribute to their goals.[53]

---

[50]Lee Sheppard and Martin Sullivan, "News Analysis: Multinationals Accumulate to Repatriate," *Tax Notes Today* (January 15, 2009).

[51]GAO, *Tax Policy: Tax Expenditures Deserve More Scrutiny*, GAO/GGD/AIMD-94-122 (Washington, D.C.: June 3, 1994), and *Government Performance and Accountability: Tax Expenditures Represent a Substantial Federal Commitment and Need to Be Reexamined*, GAO-05-690 (Washington, D.C.: Sept. 23, 2005).

[52]GAO, *Managing For Results: Executive Branch Should More Fully Implement the GPRA Modernization Act to Address Pressing Governance Challenges*, GAO-13-518 (Washington, D.C.: June 26, 2013).

[53]See also OMB Circular No. A-11 (July 2013).

Evaluation of Graduated Corporate Income Tax Rate Schedule

① What is the tax expenditure's purpose and is it being achieved?

The Graduated Corporate Income Tax Rate Schedule's Purpose Is Viewed as Supporting Small Businesses, but It May Not Be Well Targeted to That Purpose

The purpose of the graduated corporate income tax rate schedule has generally been described in the academic literature and by tax experts as supporting small businesses by reducing their tax burden. The tax expenditure benefits businesses that organize under Subchapter C of the IRC, "C corporations," by taxing their income at reduced tax rates when the income falls beneath certain limits. To the extent that small corporations have income beneath these limits, they could benefit from the reduced rates.[54]

Some rationales for providing this tax benefit to smaller businesses include encouraging entrepreneurship, innovation, and small business growth and employment. It has been argued in some academic literature that the greater after-tax income may make the small businesses more attractive to investors, and may alleviate a lack of access to capital that small businesses experience due to limited information on their business model or profit potential. Similar justifications have been made for providing benefits through other federal programs, such as federal small business loan programs. CRS' tax expenditure compendium details how

---

[54]The benefit that the graduated corporate income tax rates provide is taken back in the form of higher rates when the corporation's income exceeds the graduated rate income range.

the graduated corporate income tax rate schedule has developed and changed legislatively over time.[55]

Evidence is mixed on whether the lower corporate tax rates provided by the graduated rate schedule increases business formation.[56] Some research shows that, although only a small number of start-up companies initially form as C corporations, when and if these businesses generate profits, they have an incentive to incorporate so that these profits are taxed at lower corporate tax rates. However, other research has also indicated that incentives can produce the opposite effect. Businesses are less likely to incorporate if corporate tax rates are high, compared to individual tax rates, and instead may choose another form of business entity that is taxed under the individual tax rates.[57] In contrast, businesses with losses will typically prefer not to incorporate so that these losses can be deducted from other higher taxed personal income. Research has also shown that in 2007 a majority of unincorporated small businesses faced a marginal tax rate of 10 to 25 percent, making the rates they paid comparable to those of the graduated corporate income tax rates.[58] IRS data have also shown that the number of businesses that organize themselves as C corporations has declined, while those organizing as S corporations and partnerships have been rising in the past decade. See figure 3.

[55]U.S. Congress, Senate Committee on the Budget, *Tax Expenditures: Compendium of Background Material on Individual Provisions*, S. Prt. 112-45, prepared by CRS (Washington, D.C.: December 2012).

[56]See Simeon Djankov, Tim Ganser, Caralee McLiesh, Rita Ramalho, and Andrei Shleifer, "The Effect of Corporate Taxes on Investment and Entrepreneurship," *American Economic Journal: Macroeconomics*, vol. 2 (July 2010); and Julie Berry Cullen and Roger H. Gordon, "Taxes and entrepreneurial risk-taking: Theory and evidence for the U.S," *Journal of Public Economics*, vol. 91 (2007).

[57]Asli Demirguc-Kunt, Inessa Love, and Vojislav Maksimovic, "Business Environment and the Incorporation Decision," *Journal of Banking and Finance*, vol. 30 (2006).

[58]Matthew J. Knittel and Susan C. Nelson, "How Would Small Business Owners Fare Under a Business Entity Tax," *National Tax Journal*, vol. 64 (December 2011).

Figure 3: Number of Returns by Form of Business, Tax Year 1986-2008

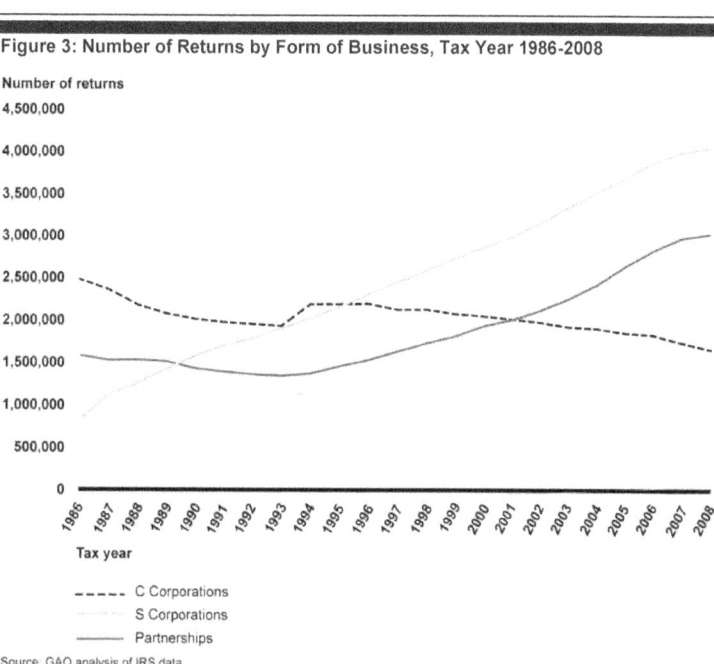

Number of returns

Source: GAO analysis of IRS data

Evidence from aggregated corporate tax return data suggests that the graduated corporate income tax rate schedule may not be well targeted at supporting small businesses. As table 2 indicates, some corporations that may not be considered small businesses claimed one of the graduated rates and received the tax benefit. For example, as table 2 shows, about 23 percent of corporations with positive taxable income that had business receipts from between $10 million and $50 million had less than $75,000 in taxable income, and benefited from the two lowest graduated rates.[59] The use of taxable income as an indicator of the size of a business may include businesses that are large by other indicators, such as total assets.

---

[59]These data represent a snapshot of IRS data, and may not be representative of trends before and after the economic recession that occurred from December 2007 to June 2009.

Table 2: Percentage of Corporations with Positive Taxable Income by Taxable Income and Size of Business Receipts, 2010

Size of business receipts	First $50,000 (15 percent)	$50,000 - $75,000 (25 percent)	$75,000 - $100,000 (34 percent)	Over $100,000 (34 percent or more)
Under $25,000	90.5%	3.3%	1.3%	4.9%
$25,000 under $100,000	95.3%	3.3%	0.6%	0.9%
$100,000 under $250,000	89.4%	5.6%	2.6%	2.4%
$250,000 under $500,000	83.6%	6.5%	5.0%	4.9%
$500,000 under $1,000,000	79.5%	10.0%	3.2%	7.2%
$1,000,000 under $2,500,000	68.8%	12.2%	5.9%	13.1%
$2,500,000 under $5,000,000	52.4%	13.0%	6.7%	28.0%
$5,000,000 under $10,000,000	31.0%	13.1%	7.6%	48.2%
$10,000,000 under $50,000,000	16.3%	6.2%	5.2%	72.4%
$50,000,000 under $100,000,000	4.4%	1.7%	2.2%	91.8%
$100,000,000 under $250,000,000	0.9%	0.9%	0.7%	97.5%
$250,000,000 and over	0.2%	0.2%	0.0%	99.7%

Source: GAO analysis of Internal Revenue Service Statistics of Income Corporate Tax File Data estimates, tax year 2010.

Notes: Data on the number of corporations are from IRS SOI corporate file and include active corporations that filed a return on forms 1120, 1120-F, 1120-L, and 1120-PC, but not forms 1120S, 1120-REIT, and 1120-RIC. The coefficient of variation for the estimates can be found in table 4, see appendix III.

Neither Treasury nor IRS has established performance measures for the graduated corporate income tax rate schedule to measure its effect, and whether it is achieving its purpose. As we previously found, most agencies have not focused on identifying the contributions tax expenditures make towards agency goals.[60]

---

[60]We made a number of recommendations to OMB, which included that it provide guidance to agencies to identify tax expenditures that contribute to each appropriate agency goal. OMB agreed with the recommendations we made. See GAO-13-518.

Even if its purpose is achieved, is the tax expenditure good policy?

- Does the tax expenditure generate net economic benefits for society?
- Is the tax expenditure fair?
- Is the tax expenditure simple, transparent, and administrable?

Efficiency Effects of the Graduated Rates Are Disputed

Some academic literature has suggested that the graduated rates can cause inefficiency by providing relief to some corporations and not others depending on their taxable income. The economy is less efficient if the rates divert resources from one type of corporation to another based on tax considerations, rather than how productively the corporations use the resources. Other sources of potential inefficiency include the incentive provided by the graduated rates for small businesses to form as C corporations to take advantage of lower corporate rates, compared to those of individual tax rates. A Treasury study found that higher differentials between corporate and non-corporate tax rates increased the likelihood that a firm will convert from C to S corporation status after the Tax Reform Act of 1986.[61] In this case, small businesses may choose an organizational form that they would not have selected without the tax incentive, suggesting that this may not be the most productive way for them to organize their operations.[62]

The graduated rates could be justified on efficiency grounds if, from society's point of view, without the incentive too few small businesses are formed given their potential for profit and innovation. It has been argued by some research that small businesses need support because they provide a disproportionate share of innovation and net job creation. However, more recent research has shown that a small number of new businesses may generate most of the innovation and net job creation. If this is the case, targeted federal support for certain small businesses may

---

[61]Treasury, *Taxes and Corporate Choice of Organizational Form* (Washington, D.C.: 1997).

[62]The effect of graduated rates on organizational form is difficult to determine because, in part, businesses have a variety of organizational forms available that affect their tax liabilities. For example, besides C corporations, they can organize as "pass-through" entities such as partnerships and S corporations that pay the individual tax rate and avoid the double tax on corporate dividends.

be more effective than graduated rates that apply to all corporations with less than a certain amount taxable income.[63]

The magnitude of the efficiency effects of the graduated rates has not been estimated, but experts agree that the effect of reducing or eliminating the rates will depend on how the change is implemented. For example, reducing or eliminating the rates without making similar changes to individual tax rates may motivate companies to change organizational form—from C corporations to "pass-through" entities like S corporations and partnerships—to take advantage of the differences between corporate and individual income tax rates.

2   **Even if its purpose is achieved, is the tax expenditure good policy?**

• Does the tax expenditure generate net economic benefits for society?
• **Is the tax expenditure fair?**
• Is the tax expenditure simple, transparent, and administrable?

Informed Judgments about the Graduated Rates' Equity Require Information about Ultimate Beneficiaries

As with the deferral tax expenditures, studies that specifically estimate the distribution of the benefits from the graduated corporate income tax rate schedule are unavailable. Without these estimates, conclusions about the fairness of the tax expenditures will be hard to draw because such judgments depend on who bears the burden of the tax or receives the benefit of the tax expenditure. The ultimate beneficiaries depend on the extent that the tax provision leads people to make decisions that change the prices of goods or services. Just as in the case of the deferral tax benefit, the benefit of graduated rates may be passed on to consumers through lower prices, employees through higher wages, or to investors through higher returns.[64]

---

[63]For more details on these studies of the impact of small businesses, see CRS' recently issued comprehensive study. CRS, *Small Business Tax Benefits: Current Law and Main Arguments For and Against Them* (Washington, D.C.: Mar. 11, 2013).

[64]The question of who receives the benefit of the tax expenditure—referred to as the incidence of the benefit —is explored in more detail in GAO-13-167SP.

• Does the tax expenditure generate net economic benefits for society?
• Is the tax expenditure fair?
• Is the tax expenditure simple, transparent, and administrable?

The Graduated Rates Likely Add Little Complexity to Determing Tax Liability But Some Evidence of Tax Planning Has Been Found

Although we did not find any estimates that isolate the compliance and administrative costs associated with the graduated rates, both costs are likely to be relatively low. IRS officials could not highlight any administrative or compliance issues involved with administering the graduated corporate income tax rate schedule. They said that applying the graduated corporate income rate schedule for a particular taxpayer is primarily a computational issue, and does not present much uncertainty to taxpayers in determining their tax liabilities. However, IRS research has found some evidence that corporations' taxable income tends to cluster below rate changes introduced by the tax rate brackets. The research found that if the tax net income of corporations in their sample of Schedule M-3 filers (generally those with assets of at least $10 million) from tax years 2004 through 2008 rose 5 percent, a substantial number of corporations would face higher marginal tax rates.[65] This clustering of filers around certain tax rates may be the result of tax planning that increases compliance costs.

The compliance and administrative costs of the graduated rates have not been estimated separately from the costs of complying with and administering all the provisions of the corporate income tax. However, estimates of the total compliance burden of small businesses may give some context to the compliance costs associated with graduated rates. A 2007 study of businesses with assets of less than $10 million in 2002 found that small businesses initially face significant fixed compliance

---

[65]Tax net income represents a firm's taxable income before subtracting any net operating loss carryforward or special deductions and is most closely comparable to domestic pre-tax book income. The most dramatic changes occurred in corporations currently in the zero-, 25- , 34- , and 38-percent tax brackets, all of which face a different marginal tax rate from a 5-percent increase in tax net income. See IRS, *The Distribution of Corporate Income: Tabulations from the Schedule M-3, 2004-2008*, SOI Bulletin (Washington, D.C.: Spring 2012).

costs, which increase at a decreasing rate as the business grows.[66] However, the specific administrative and compliance costs of the graduated rates may not be a large part of these costs compared with other, more complicated provisions of the tax code.

| 3 | How does the tax expenditure relate to other federal programs? |

Graduated Rates Are Related to a Number of Spending Programs but the Relative Effectiveness of the Tax Expenditure Has Not Been Assessed

Our prior work on corporate tax expenditures found no related federal spending program sharing the same reported purpose as the graduated rates of supporting small businesses that adopt the corporate form of legal organization.[67] However, there are federal spending programs that share, at least in part, the similar purpose of supporting entrepreneurs and small businesses. In prior work, we identified 52 programs at the U.S. Departments of Agriculture, Commerce, and Housing and Urban Development, and the Small Business Administration, which all overlap with at least one other program in terms of the type of assistance they are authorized to offer, and the type of entrepreneur they are authorized to serve.[68]

Changes in the graduated rates are generally part of proposals to reduce the overall corporate tax rate which are discussed in the context of tax reform. The issue of whether the tax expenditure could be better designed to target small business or spending or non-tax policies that

---

[66]See Donald DeLuca, John Guyton, Wu-Lang Lee, John O'Hare, and Scott Stilmar, *Aggregate Estimates of Small Business Taxpayer Compliance Burden*, IRS Research Bulletin (2007).

[67]See GAO-13-339.

[68]GAO, *Entrepreneurial Assistance: Opportunities Exist to Improve Programs Collaboration, Data Track, and Performance Management*, GAO-12-819 (Washington, D.C.: Aug. 23, 2012).

GAO-13-789 Corporate Tax Expenditures

support small businesses may be preferable but has not been part of the discussion.

Moving to a Flat Corporate Income Tax Rate of 35 Percent Would Have Relatively Modest Consequences for the Federal Budget

According to JCT estimates produced in 2011 and reported by CBO, moving to a single corporate rate of 35 percent would have raised $1.5 billion in 2012.[69] This estimate is based on a specific proposal to change the tax code, and includes behavioral responses by taxpayers to the tax change. JCT and Treasury also annually calculate tax expenditure estimates that do not account for how taxpayer behavior may change when a tax expenditure is altered. Because they do not account for these behavioral changes or interactions with other tax provisions, the tax expenditure estimates available for the graduated rates do not represent the amount of revenue that would be gained if these rates were repealed. However, as mentioned above in the case of deferral, these estimates can indicate how revenue losses may be changing over time. As shown in figure 4, estimated tax revenue losses from the graduated corporate income tax rate schedule have decreased in the past decade. From 1998 through 2012, estimated tax revenue losses fell from $7.3 billion to $4.3 billion in constant 2012 dollars. The estimated fiscal year 2012 loss was 3 percent of all estimated revenue losses from corporate tax expenditures ($147 billion). The estimate was equal to 1.8 percent of corporate tax revenue in 2012.

---

[69]From 2012 to 2016, the revenue effects of this option would be $12.1 billion. The staff of the JCT prepared most of the revenue estimates in CBO's report. See CBO, *Reducing the Deficit: Spending and Revenue Options* (Washington, D.C.: Mar. 10, 2011).

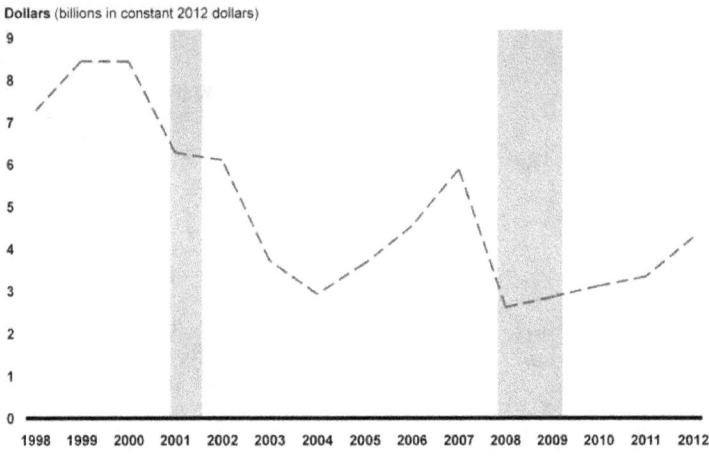

Figure 4: Estimated Federal Tax Revenue Losses Due to Graduated Corporate Income Tax Rate Schedule, Reported by Treasury, 1998-2012

Dollars (billions in constant 2012 dollars)

Fiscal year

U.S. economic recession

— — — Graduated Corporate Income Tax Rate tax expenditure revenue loss estimates

Source: GAO analysis of OMB budget, fiscal years 2000-2014.

The decrease in figure 4 may be due, in part, to less companies incorporating as C corporations, which we highlighted above.

No Consensus Exists on Which Agency Should Evaluate the Graduated Corporate Tax Rate Schedule

As in the case of the deferral tax expenditures, no agency has been tasked with evaluating the graduated corporate income tax rate schedule. In June 2013, we made a number of recommendations to OMB, including that it should provide guidance to agencies to identify tax expenditures that contribute to each appropriate agency goal.[70] In July 2013, OMB released guidance that directs agencies to identify tax expenditures that contribute to their goals.[71]

Agency and Third Party Comments and Our Evaluation

We provided a draft of this report to the Secretary of the Treasury and the Commissioner of Internal Revenue for comment. We also asked the Joint Committee on Taxation (JCT) and all external experts we interviewed to review a draft of this report. Treasury, IRS, JCT, and external experts provided technical comments that were incorporated, as appropriate.

We sent copies of this report to the Secretary of the Treasury, to the Commissioner of Internal Revenue, and other interested parties. This report will also be available at no charge on GAO's website at http://www.gao.gov.

---

[70]GAO, *Managing For Results: Executive Branch Should More Fully Implement the GPRA Modernization Act to Address Pressing Governance Challenges*, GAO-13-518 (Washington, D.C.: June 26, 2013).

[71]See also OMB Circular No. A-11 (July 2013).

If you have any questions on this report, please contact me at (202) 512-9110 or whitej@gao.gov. Contact points for our offices of Congressional Relations and Public Affairs may be found on the last page of this report. Key contributors to this are listed in appendix IV.

James R. White
Director, Tax Issues
Strategic Issues

Appendix I: Objectives, Scope, and Methodology

This report uses our tax expenditures evaluation guide to determine what is known about following three tax expenditures: (1) the deferral of income for controlled foreign corporations; (2) deferred taxes for certain financial firms on income earned overseas; and (3) the graduated corporate income tax rate. Because deferred taxes for certain financial firms on income earned overseas is a special case of the treatment of foreign source income of all controlled foreign corporations, our first section of the report focuses our discussion on the more general case of all controlled foreign corporations using deferral. Our second section of the report covers the graduated corporate income tax rate schedule. For both sections of the report, we cover the five questions outlined in our guide and listed below to determine what is known about each tax expenditure. We highlight what questions we are answering for each tax expenditure at the beginning of each section of the report.

GAO Tax Expenditure Evaluation Guide

To evaluate the three tax expenditures above, we applied our tax expenditure evaluation guide, which was issued in November 2012.[1] The guide outlines a series of questions and sub-questions that can be used to evaluate tax expenditures. The five primary questions and sub-questions outlined in the guide are:

1. What is the tax expenditure's purpose and is being achieved?

    *   What is the tax expenditure's intended purpose?

    *   Have performance measures been established to monitor success in achieving the tax expenditure's intended purpose?

    *   Does the tax expenditure succeed in achieving its intended purpose?

2. Even if its purpose is achieved, is the tax expenditure good policy?

    *   Does the tax expenditure generate net economic benefits for society?

    *   Is the tax expenditure fair?

---

[1] GAO, *Tax Expenditures: Background and Evaluation Criteria and Questions*, GAO-13-167SP (Washington, D.C.: Nov. 29, 2012)

- Is the tax expenditure simple, transparent, and administrable?

3. How does the tax expenditure relate to other federal programs?

  - Does the tax expenditure contribute to a designated cross-agency priority goal?

  - Does the tax expenditure duplicate or overlap with another federal effort?

  - Is the tax expenditure being coordinated with other federal activities?

  - Would an alternative to the tax expenditure more effectively achieve its intended purpose?

4. What are the consequences for the federal budget of the tax expenditure?

  - Are there budget effects not captured by Treasury's or the Joint Committee on Taxation's tax expenditure estimates?

  - Are there options for limiting the tax expenditure's revenue loss?

5. How should evaluation of the tax expenditure be managed?

  - What agency or agencies should evaluate the tax expenditure?

  - When should the tax expenditure be evaluated?

  - What data are needed to evaluate the tax expenditure?

The guide's questions cover a number of different policy objectives. Sometimes, these objectives compete. This report provides information responsive to the questions, but does not attempt to balance the different objectives or make recommendations. Rather, policymakers are better positioned to judge how competing policy objectives should be weighed. As we note in our tax expenditure evaluation guide, it is not a "one size fits all" framework for evaluating tax expenditures. We used reasonable judgment in applying the guide's questions and concepts to evaluate the three tax expenditures. In some instances, we focused our discussion on certain questions in the guide because they were more relevant to the tax expenditures we were evaluating, while devoting less discussion to others that were more technical in nature.

- Question 1 above covers the tax expenditure's intended purpose and if it is being achieved. Since the purpose of the deferral tax expenditures is unclear, we did not address the sub-questions related to whether the deferral tax expenditures achieve their intended purpose, and if performance measures have been established.

- For question 2 above, our discussion of the deferral tax expenditures and criteria for good policy also includes question 3 above which covers alternatives to the tax expenditures, as there is a natural relation to alternative proposals and how they may affect the criteria outlined in question 2.

To the extent that we use our tax expenditure evaluation guide in the future on other tax expenditures, the structure and focus of future reports may differ from how it is presented in this report. To determine what is known about the deferral tax expenditures and the graduated corporate income tax rate schedule by answering the five questions listed above, we reviewed the following sources:

- Our previous work on tax expenditures, tax reform, tax policy and administration, duplication, overlap, and fragmentation, and results-oriented government and program evaluation.

- Previous work by the Congressional Research Service (CRS), the Congressional Budget Office (CBO), the Joint Committee on Taxation (JCT), the Department of the Treasury (Treasury), and the Internal Revenue Service (IRS).

- Legislation, statutes, and regulations.

- Academic and scholarly research on the tax expenditures and corporate taxation. To identify academic literature, we searched terms and certain authors in a number of academic literature databases, such as ProQuest, Econlit, and Social SciSearch. We reviewed and identified academic literature cited in CRS' tax expenditure compendium, and a comprehensive study by JCT on foreign direct investment.[2] We reviewed articles published in the National Tax

---

[2]U.S. Congress, Senate Committee on the Budget, *Tax Expenditures: Compendium of Background Material on Individual Provisions*, S. Prt. 111-58, prepared by CRS (Washington, D.C.: December 2010) and U.S. Congress, Senate Committee on Finance, *Economic Efficiency and Structural Analyses of Alternative U.S. Tax Policies For Foreign Direct Investment.* Prepared by JCT (Washington, D.C.: June 2008).

Journal and asked Treasury, IRS, and the external experts we interviewed for recommendations on articles to review. We also interviewed Treasury and IRS officials, and external experts affiliated with CRS and two universities, who specialize in the U.S. corporate income tax system. The results from these interviews are not generalizable.

- Treasury tax expenditure estimates for fiscal years 1998 through 2012, and estimates by JCT on the revenue effects of making changes to the tax expenditures in our scope.[3] To identify how the deferral and graduated corporate income tax rate schedule tax expenditures have changed in terms of their aggregate estimated revenue losses, we analyzed tax expenditure estimates developed by the Treasury and reported by the Office of Management and Budget in the Federal Budget's Analytical Perspectives for fiscal years 1998 through 2012.[4] We converted all tax expenditure estimates for each fiscal year into 2012 constant dollars to adjust for inflation. We did so by using the chain price indexes reported in the fiscal year 2014 federal budget. While sufficiently reliable as a gauge of general magnitude, summing tax expenditure estimates do not take into account any interactions between tax expenditures. In addition, tax expenditure estimates do not incorporate any behavioral responses. Thus, they do not represent the revenue amount that would be gained if a specific tax expenditure was repealed. To identify JCT estimates of the revenue effects of making changes to the tax expenditures in our scope, we reviewed CBO's latest report that outlines spending and revenue options. These options outline a number of changes to the tax expenditures in our scope with accompanying estimates from JCT.[5] Its revenue-effect estimates take into account a number of behavioral changes, unlike the tax expenditure estimates that Treasury and JCT complete. These include possible behavioral

---

[3]We chose 1998 as the first year as that was the first year Treasury estimated revenue losses for deferred taxes for financial firms on certain income earned overseas since the exception was eliminated in 1986. See 26 U.S.C. § 954(h), which was added by the Taxpayer Relief Act of 1997, Pub. L. No 105-34 § 1175 (Aug. 5, 1997).

[4]Treasury estimates the portion of revenue losses associated with corporate or individual taxpayers for each tax expenditure in its list. However, all three tax expenditures in the scope of our report only have tax expenditure estimates for corporate taxpayers.

[5]See CBO, *Reducing the Deficit: Spending and Revenue Options* (Washington, D.C.: Mar. 10, 2011).

changes in: (1) corporate dividends and retained earnings; (2) the corporate capital structure; (3) corporate equity valuations; (4) repatriations of deferred foreign income; and (5) business entity choice.[6]

- Data estimates from IRS Statistics of Income (SOI) Corporate Tax File, 2010, the most recent year available at the time of our work, and Bureau of Economic Analysis (BEA) data on corporate profits from 1987 through 2012. We requested estimates from the IRS SOI 2010 Corporate Tax File on the number of C corporations by their corporate income tax bracket, and a measurement of their size—in this case—business receipts. Data compiled by IRS SOI are based on a stratified random sample of 63,630 corporate income tax returns for 2010 from corporations that end their corporate year from July 1, 2010, through June 30, 2011. These estimates are subject to sampling errors. The margin of error is based on a 95-percent confidence interval. For our report, IRS SOI provided data on C corporations, which include active corporations filing tax forms 1120, 1120-F, 1120-L, and 1120-PC. Data are not included for "pass-through" entities, which file on forms 1120S, 1120-REIT, and 1120-RIC. We used business receipts as our measurement of size and used IRS' breakout for the different sizes of business receipts. We also obtained data from IRS on the number of different types of business form entities (C corporations, S corporations, and partnerships) from 1986 to 2008. We also analyzed data from BEA on corporate profits by industry from 1987 to 2012. To determine how the composition of U.S. corporate profits have changed over time, we took a ratio of the amount of profit earned by U.S. corporations abroad compared to the total amount of profits earned by U.S. corporations. This analysis was based on a similar analysis used in academic literature.[7]

To assess the reliability of the data and estimates, we reviewed agency documentation, interviewed agency officials, and reviewed our prior reports that have used the data and estimates. We determined that Treasury, JCT, BEA, and IRS data and estimates were sufficiently reliable for our purposes. However, the IRS SOI corporate sample may not provide a precise estimate of the number of taxpayers claiming a tax

---

[6]See JCT, *Su⬚⬚a⬚⬚of ⬚cono⬚ic ⬚ode⬚s and ⬚sti⬚ating ⬚⬚actices of the Staff of the ⬚oint ⬚o⬚⬚ittee on ⬚a⬚ation* (Washington, D.C.: Sept. 19, 2011).

[7]Mihir A. Desai and James R. Hines Jr., "Old Rules and New Realities: Corporate Tax Policy in a Global Setting," *⬚ationa⬚⬚a⬚⬚ou⬚na⬚,* vol. 57 (December 2004).

expenditure when the number of taxpayers is very small. We conducted our work from April to September 2013 in accordance with all sections of GAO's Quality Assurance Framework that are relevant to our objectives. The framework requires that we plan and perform the engagement to obtain sufficient and appropriate evidence to meet our stated objectives, and to discuss any limitations in our work. We believe that the information and data obtained and the analysis conducted provide a reasonable basis for any findings and conclusions in this product.

Appendix II: Comparison of Territorial and Worldwide Corporate Income Tax Systems

Many proposals for changing the way the current U.S. system taxes foreign source income are detailed and complex.[1] In general, however, they involve redesigning the current system to more resemble a pure worldwide or a pure territorial system. The basic designs of the three systems being considered as alternatives are the following:

- The current worldwide system with deferral. Foreign active business income is taxed when repatriated as dividends to the U.S. This system has a foreign tax credit limited to the U.S. tax liability on foreign source income, and certain anti-deferral provisions like Subpart F.

- A territorial system that uses a dividend exemption. The dividends derived from foreign active business income can be repatriated without U.S. tax. This system would continue to tax Subpart F income as do most countries with territorial systems.

- A worldwide system with full inclusion. The current worldwide system is retained, but deferral of foreign active business income is eliminated.

The current system serves as a benchmark against which to compare the alternatives. When applying the criteria of a good tax system, the territorial and worldwide systems with full inclusion are examined for their effect on efficiency, equity, and complexity, and their relativity to the effects of the current system. Figure 5 illustrates how the basic design of the full inclusion worldwide system and the territorial system affects the taxes that corporations pay.

---

[1]Harry Grubert and Rosanne Altshuler, *Fixing the System: An Analysis of Alternative Proposals for the Reform of International Tax*, Working Papers Series (Apr. 1, 2013) and CRS, *Reform of U.S. International Taxation: Alternatives* (Washington, D.C.: Dec. 27, 2012).

⬚igure 5⬚Exa⬚ p⬚e o⬚⬚ orld⬚ide and Territoria⬚Corporate ⬚n⬚o⬚ e Tax ⬚⬚ste⬚ s

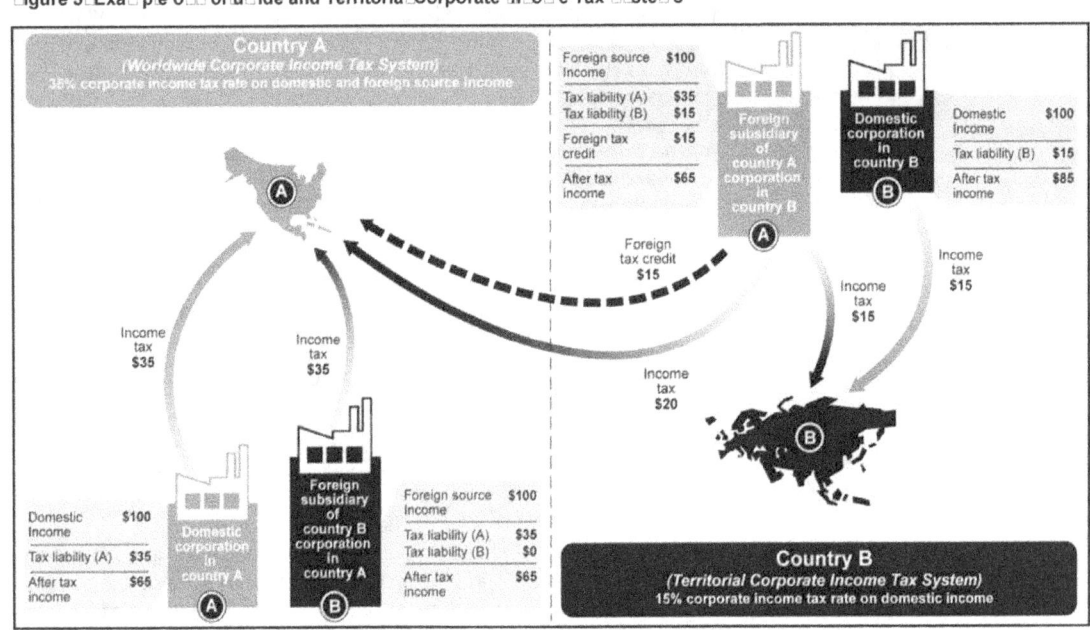

Source: GAO analysis.

As shown in figure 5, Country A has a worldwide tax system that taxes income of its domestic corporations, and that of foreign corporations earned within its borders at the same 35-percent rate. The domestic corporation and the subsidiary of the foreign corporation each pay $35 in taxes to Country A. Additionally, Country A taxes the income of the foreign subsidiaries of its corporations at the same 35-percent rate. However, in this case, it provides a credit for taxes paid to the country in which the subsidiary operates. The subsidiary gets a $15 credit for the tax it pays to Country B, and subtracts this amount from the $35 tax liability that it owes its home Country A. The total tax paid by the subsidiary is $15 to Country B plus the $20 net tax that it pays at home for an overall tax of $35. For the worldwide system, taxes paid are the same for corporations operating within Country A, and for its corporations operating abroad.

In a territorial system, income is taxed only by the country in which it is earned. In figure 5, Country B has a territorial system that imposes a 15-

percent tax on corporations that operate within its borders. The domestic
corporation and the subsidiary of the foreign corporation remit the same
tax payment of $15 to Country B on $100 of income earned there. Unlike
the worldwide system, the territorial system imposes no tax on the income
of the foreign subsidiaries of its own corporations. For the territorial
system, taxes paid are equal for corporations operating within Country B,
but differ for corporations operating across borders.

As discussed above, the experts we interviewed agreed and economic
theory suggests that any corporate tax system's overall effect on
efficiency depends on its relative effect on different types of investment
decisions. The full inclusion system is likely to increase investment
location efficiency relative to the current and territorial systems. Under the
current system, investment abroad has a lower tax cost when repatriation
of the foreign source income is deferred. Full inclusion would eliminate
this tax advantage, and would be more consistent with efficient location
decisions. When the foreign tax rate is lower than the U.S. tax rate,
domestic corporations under full inclusion pay taxes on income earned at
home and abroad at the same rate—the U.S. tax rate. The system does
not provide incentives either to invest abroad or at home (i.e. it is neutral
with respect to the location of investment).[2] The territorial system, on the
other hand, may increase investment location inefficiencies by making the
location incentives that arise when countries adopt different tax rates
permanent.

However, as previously noted in this report, these inefficiencies may be
offset to some extent by improved ownership efficiencies and reduced
incentives to move corporate residences abroad. Corporations operating
under a territorial system pay the same tax rate on income from their
operations in each country. This would eliminate any tax advantage that
would allow a less efficient owner in that country to acquire the more
productive corporation. While the full inclusion system may not distort
location decisions, it may distort decisions about who owns the foreign
subsidiaries. Some advocates of the territorial system argue that

---

[2]If the U.S. tax rate is lower than the foreign tax rate, the U.S. system, which limits the
foreign tax credit to the U.S. tax liability on the foreign income, discourages investment
abroad. See Organisation for Economic Co-operation and Development, ⬜a⬜ ⬜ffects on
⬜o⬜eign Di⬜ect ⬜nvest⬜ ent: Recent ⬜vidence and ⬜o⬜ic⬜ ⬜na⬜sis⬜⬜a⬜ ⬜o⬜ic⬜ Stud⬜ ⬜o⬜⬜⬜
(2007)⬜

efficiency gains from eliminating this ownership distortion can offset any efficiency losses from distorted location decisions.

The experts whom we interviewed and the research that we reviewed agreed that both the territorial and full inclusion systems eliminate efficiency cost from the lockout effect that exists under the current system. Full inclusion eliminates the lockout effect by making foreign-earned income taxable without repatriation. The territorial system eliminates the lockout effect by making foreign-earned income tax free, whether or not they are repatriated. The effect of the lockout's elimination could be significant because of possibly large efficiency costs due to growing accumulations of income abroad.

Some research has suggested that income-shifting incentives should be significantly reduced under full inclusion, but may be increased under the territorial system. Researchers have found evidence of extensive income shifting under the current system.[3] Full inclusion nearly eliminates incentives for income shifting because corporations pay the same rate under full inclusion, regardless of where the income is located and the timing of its repatriation.[4] The territorial system, on the other hand, would likely increase the incentive to shift income to lower-tax countries because income earned abroad would be exempt from being taxed, even when repatriated.

The relative effects of the alternatives on compliance and administrative burden depend on the specifics of their design. As described above, the current system is complex, and imposes compliance and administrative burden by requiring extensive calculations and adjustments involving foreign tax credits, sourcing rules for income and expenses, and transfer-pricing rules to limit income shifting. Some research has shown that, while a full inclusion system would reduce the benefits and scope for income shifting, it would also retain some of the current system's burden, such as the foreign tax credit and sourcing rules for income and expenses. The territorial system, by increasing income-shifting incentives, may require

---

[3]Harry Grubert. "Foreign Taxes and the Growing Share of U.S. Multinational Company Income Abroad: Profits, Not Sales, Are Being Globalized," *National Tax Journal,* vol. 65 (June 2012). The author argues that income shifting may be growing due to tax-planning opportunities that were increased by check-the-box-rules in 1997.

[4]The incentive to shift income disappears, except for companies that have excess credits.

provisions to protect the tax base that can add considerable complexity to the tax code. The degree of complexity relative to the current system will depend in part on how much of the current rules are maintained or expanded in the new system. However, because both the territorial and full inclusion systems remove any incentive to delay repatriation, they would eliminate compliance and administrative burden due to the repatriation tax planning that occurs under the current system.

Based on the research and revenue estimates we reviewed, the revenue raised by each system depends on the specifics of its design. How much of the potential worldwide tax revenue a country gets depends on its tax system's incentives to relocate income to a lower tax rate country. Some research has noted that under full inclusion, the corporation has no incentive to relocate income to a lower tax country unless it has excess foreign tax credits. However, under a territorial tax system, the corporation has an incentive to move income to a lower tax rate foreign country. Based on these incentives, it would appear that revenue for the home country is likely to decrease when a country moves from a worldwide to a territorial system. However, the relative effects on revenue ultimately depend on the details of the design. For example, some features of a territorial system's design are implemented specifically to limit revenue losses. Under its territorial system, Japan imposes a per-country minimum tax, which means that corporations will lack incentives to locate income in a country with a tax rate below the minimum.[5] Other features of a tax system that affect revenues include changes in income and expense allocation rules that would increase foreign source income attributed to the home country under a territorial system.

---

[5]GAO, *⬚nte⬚nationa⬚ ⬚a⬚ation: Stud⬚ ⬚ount⬚ies ⬚hat ⬚⬚e⬚pt ⬚o⬚eign⬚Sou⬚ce ⬚nco⬚ e ⬚ace ⬚o⬚p⬚iance Ris⬚s and ⬚u⬚dens Si⬚i⬚a⬚to ⬚hose in the ⬚nited States⬚*GAO-09-934 (Washington, D.C.: Sept. 15, 2009).

Table 3: Number of Corporate Taxpayers by Taxable Income and Size of Business Receipts, 2010

Size of business receipts	No taxable income	First $50,000 (15 percent)	$50,000-$75,000 (25 percent)	$75,000-$100,000 (34 percent)	$100,000-$335,000 (39 percent)	$335,000-$10,000,000 (34 percent)	$10,000,000-$15,000,000 (35 percent)	$15,000,000-$18,333,333 (38 percent)	Over $18,333,333 (35 percent)
Under $25,000	353,943	67,381	2,427	996	2,471	1,107	14	11	43
$25,000 under $100,000	181,917	65,036	2,251	383	440	166	**	**	3
$100,000 under $250,000	183,569	68,107	4,304	1,945	1,753	83	**	**	**
$250,000 under $500,000	137,421	51,575	3,980	3,071	2,702	340	**	**	**
$500,000 under $1,000,000	116,640	48,000	6,043	1,948	3,804	560	3	**	0
$1,000,000 under $2,500,000	101,849	46,875	8,325	4,014	6,868	2,027	6	**	3
$2,500,000 under $5,000,000	43,176	18,972	4,701	2,416	6,749	3,369	4	**	6
$5,000,000 under $10,000,000	21,690	7,560	3,204	1,860	6,772	4,955	9	3	10
$10,000,000 under $50,000,000	19,801	4,014	1,531	1,280	6,112	11,455	152	56	98
$50,000,000 under $100,000,000	2,934	167	63	86	479	2,649	190	50	150
$100,000,000 under $250,000,000	2,081	24	23	19	127	1,564	292	135	457
$250,000,000 and over	2,140	5	5	0	26	662	235	111	2,112

Source: IRS Statistics of Income (SOI) Corporate Tax File data estimates, tax year 2010.

Note: Data on the number of corporations are from IRS SOI Corporate Tax File, and include active corporations that filed a return on forms 1120, 1120-F, 1120-L, and 1120-PC, but not forms 1120S, 1120-REIT, and 1120-RIC.

** Data have been combined with data in a lower size class to avoid disclosure for specific corporations.

Appendix ▢▢▢▢▢ ▢tatisti▢s o▢n▢o▢e ▢ata on
t▢e ▢u▢▢er o▢C Corporations ▢▢Taxa▢e
▢n▢o▢e and ▢i▢e o▢▢usiness ▢e▢eipts▢▢▢1▢

Ta▢e ▢▢Coe▢▢i▢ient o▢▢ariation Ca▢▢u▢ations ▢or Tota▢s in Ta▢e 3

▢i▢e o▢ ▢usiness ▢e▢eipts	▢o taxa▢e in▢o▢e	▢irst ▢5▢▢▢▢ ▢15 per▢ent▢	▢5▢▢▢- ▢75▢▢▢ ▢5 per▢ent▢	▢75▢▢▢- ▢1▢▢▢▢▢ ▢3▢ per▢ent▢	▢1▢▢▢▢▢- ▢335▢▢▢ ▢39 per▢ent▢	▢335▢▢▢- ▢1▢▢▢▢▢▢ ▢3▢ per▢ent▢	▢1▢▢▢▢▢▢- ▢15▢▢▢▢▢▢ ▢35 per▢ent▢	▢15▢▢▢▢▢▢- ▢18▢333▢333 ▢38 per▢ent▢	O▢er ▢18▢333▢333 ▢35 per▢ent▢	▢o▢ Tota▢
Under $25,000	4.28	10.70	57.40	89.45	56.67	81.84	205.37	733.58	16.50	3.80
$25,000 under $100,000	6.31	10.90	59.55	139.22	132.98	211.65	—	—	51.64	5.27
$100,000 under $250,000	6.27	10.65	43.08	64.04	67.05	291.45	—	—	—	5.15
$250,000 under $500,000	7.35	12.28	44.76	51.01	54.03	150.34	—	—	—	5.99
$500,000 under $1,000,000	8.02	12.74	36.32	63.94	45.62	115.06	—	—	—	6.39
$1,000,000 under $2,500,000	8.60	12.89	30.84	44.47	33.87	61.07	0.00	—	51.64	6.53
$2,500,000 under $5,000,000	13.32	20.38	41.05	57.13	33.90	45.50	0.00	—	44.70	9.73
$5,000,000 under $10,000,000	18.60	32.31	49.65	65.15	33.87	36.80	53.95	89.27	34.62	12.71
$10,000,000 under $50,000,000	18.46	44.14	71.52	77.80	35.50	23.86	10.89	17.40	12.33	12.39
$50,000,000 under $100,000,000	36.36	206.26	329.60	302.03	123.58	44.41	9.75	16.27	8.9	26.00
$100,000,000 under $250,000,000	25.48	487.74	478.36	580.59	210.34	40.56	165.20	23.53	17.78	21.51
$250,000,000 and over	4.81	798.88	798.50	—	460.64	30.59	6.64	8.03	0.88	5.00

Source: GAO analysis of IRS Statistics of Income (SOI) Corporate Tax File data estimates, tax year 2010.

Note: This table contains the coefficient of variation. It is the estimate divided by the standard error. The estimate can be either a total or a percent. When the estimate is small (1 percent or 5 corporations), the coefficient of variation may be more than 100. Data on the number of corporations are from IRS SOI Corporate Tax File, and include active corporations that filed a return on forms 1120, 1120-F, 1120-L, and 1120-PC, but not forms 1120S, 1120-REIT, and 1120-RIC.

— The sample has no observations in this cell. The population may have corporations in this cell. However, we do not have sufficient information to calculate an appropriate margin of error.

Appendix IV: GAO Contact and Staff Acknowledgments

GAO Contact

James R. White, (202) 512-9110 or whitej@gao.gov.

Staff Acknowledgments

In addition to the contact name above, Kevin Daly (Assistant Director), Jason Vassilicos (Analyst-in-Charge), Elwood D. White, JoAnna Berry, Robert Gebhart, Eric Gorman, Lois Hanshaw, Benjamin Licht, Ed Nannenhorn, Karen O'Conor, Kathleen Padulchick, Robert Robinson, Stewart W. Small, Anne Stevens, and Jim Wozny all made contributions to this report.

GAO's Mission	The Government Accountability Office, the audit, evaluation, and investigative arm of Congress, exists to support Congress in meeting its constitutional responsibilities and to help improve the performance and accountability of the federal government for the American people. GAO examines the use of public funds; evaluates federal programs and policies; and provides analyses, recommendations, and other assistance to help Congress make informed oversight, policy, and funding decisions. GAO's commitment to good government is reflected in its core values of accountability, integrity, and reliability.
Obtaining Copies of GAO Reports and Testimony	The fastest and easiest way to obtain copies of GAO documents at no cost is through GAO's website (http://www.gao.gov). Each weekday afternoon, GAO posts on its website newly released reports, testimony, and correspondence. To have GAO e-mail you a list of newly posted products, go to http://www.gao.gov and select "E-mail Updates."
Order by Phone	The price of each GAO publication reflects GAO's actual cost of production and distribution and depends on the number of pages in the publication and whether the publication is printed in color or black and white. Pricing and ordering information is posted on GAO's website, http://www.gao.gov/ordering.htm. Place orders by calling (202) 512-6000, toll free (866) 801-7077, or TDD (202) 512-2537. Orders may be paid for using American Express, Discover Card, MasterCard, Visa, check, or money order. Call for additional information.
Connect with GAO	Connect with GAO on Facebook, Flickr, Twitter, and YouTube. Subscribe to our RSS Feeds or E-mail Updates. Listen to our Podcasts. Visit GAO on the web at www.gao.gov.
To Report Fraud, Waste, and Abuse in Federal Programs	Contact: Website: http://www.gao.gov/fraudnet/fraudnet.htm E-mail: fraudnet@gao.gov Automated answering system: (800) 424-5454 or (202) 512-7470
Congressional Relations	Katherine Siggerud, Managing Director, siggerudk@gao.gov, (202) 512-4400, U.S. Government Accountability Office, 441 G Street NW, Room 7125, Washington, DC 20548
Public Affairs	Chuck Young, Managing Director, youngc1@gao.gov, (202) 512-4800 U.S. Government Accountability Office, 441 G Street NW, Room 7149 Washington, DC 20548

Please Print on Recycled Paper.